Excel Shortcut Pro 2025

600+ Time-Saving Keyboard Commands to Master Excel Like a Pro — Navigate, Edit, Automate, and Format Spreadsheets Effortlessly on Windows and Mac

Nate Griffin

Contents

Basic Navigation

Shortcut	Action
Arrow Keys	Move one cell up, down, left, or right
Ctrl + Arrow Keys	Jump to edge of data region in direction
Home	Move to beginning of row
Ctrl + Home	Move to cell A1
Ctrl + End	Move to last cell with data
Page Down	Move one screen down
Page Up	Move one screen up
Alt + Page Down	Move one screen right
Alt + Page Up	Move one screen left
Ctrl + Page Down	Switch to next worksheet
Ctrl + Page Up	Switch to previous worksheet
F5	Go To a specific cell
Ctrl + G	Go To dialog box (same as F5)
Ctrl + Backspace	Scroll to the active cell
Tab	Move one cell to the right
Shift + Tab	Move one cell to the left

Shortcut	Action
Enter	Move one cell down
Shift + Enter	Move one cell up
Ctrl + Shift + Arrow	Select cells to edge of data region
Ctrl + . (period)	Move clockwise through corners of a selected range
Ctrl + ;	Insert current date
Ctrl + :	Insert current time
Ctrl + F	Find
Ctrl + H	Replace
Ctrl + L	Create a table from selected data
Ctrl + Space	Select entire column
Shift + Space	Select entire row
Ctrl + Shift + Space	Select entire worksheet (press twice for table)
Esc	Cancel current entry or exit a menu
Alt + Enter	Start a new line within a cell
Ctrl + 1	Open Format Cells dialog
Ctrl + Tab	Switch between open workbooks
Ctrl + Shift + Tab	Switch to previous open workbook

Shortcut	Action
Alt + F1	Create chart from data in current range (quick chart)
Alt + F11	Open VBA Editor
F2	Edit active cell
Shift + F2	Add or edit cell comment

Selection Techniques

These shortcuts help you **select cells, ranges, rows, columns, objects, and worksheets** more efficiently. They're especially useful for formatting, editing, and analyzing data faster.

Shortcut	Action
Shift + Arrow Keys	Extend selection one cell at a time in direction
Ctrl + Shift + Arrow Keys	Extend selection to the edge of data region
Ctrl + A	Select entire worksheet (if used in blank cell); select current region
Ctrl + Shift + Space	Select entire worksheet
Ctrl + Space	Select entire column
Shift + Space	Select entire row

Shortcut	Action
Ctrl + Shift + Home	Select from current cell to beginning of worksheet
Ctrl + Shift + End	Select from current cell to last cell with data
Ctrl + . (Period)	Cycle through corners of selected range
Ctrl + * (Asterisk)	Select current region around active cell (same as Ctrl + A if in data)
Ctrl + Shift + 8	Same as Ctrl + * – select region
Shift + Click (with mouse)	Extend selection to clicked cell
Ctrl + Click	Select multiple non-adjacent cells or ranges
Ctrl + Shift + Click	Add additional non-adjacent cells to selection
Ctrl + /	Select array formula range (in legacy arrays)
F8	Turn on Extend Selection mode
Shift + F8	Add to selection (without extending)

Shortcut	Action
Esc	Cancel selection/exit Extend Selection mode
Ctrl + \	Select cells in row that differ from active cell in selected column
Ctrl + Shift + \	Select cells in column that differ from active cell in selected row
Ctrl + 6	Show/hide objects (can be helpful for working with shapes/images)
Ctrl + 9	Hide selected rows
Ctrl + Shift + 9	Unhide rows
Ctrl + 0 (zero)	Hide selected columns
Ctrl + Shift + 0	Unhide columns (Note: may require enabling in Windows registry)
Ctrl + ~ (tilde)	Show formulas – reveals all formula cells

Cell Editing

These shortcuts help you **enter, edit, delete, and manipulate data within cells** quickly and accurately. They're perfect for both data entry and formula editing.

Shortcut	Action
F2	Edit active cell
Enter	Complete cell entry and move one cell down
Shift + Enter	Complete cell entry and move one cell up
Tab	Complete cell entry and move one cell to the right
Shift + Tab	Complete cell entry and move one cell to the left
Esc	Cancel cell entry
Backspace	Delete one character to the left within edit mode
Delete	Clear content of selected cells
Ctrl + Delete	Delete to the end of line within cell when editing

Shortcut	Action
Ctrl + Z	Undo last action
Ctrl + Y	Redo last action
Ctrl + D	Fill down — copy content/formula from cell above
Ctrl + R	Fill right — copy content/formula from cell on the left
Alt + Enter	Insert a line break within a cell
Ctrl + ;	Insert current date
Ctrl + Shift + :	Insert current time
Ctrl + Shift + "+"	Insert new cell (opens Insert dialog)
Ctrl + "-"	Delete selected cells (opens Delete dialog)
Ctrl + ' (apostrophe)	Copy formula from cell above
Ctrl + Shift + "	Copy value from cell above
Ctrl + 1	Open Format Cells dialog

Shortcut	Action
Ctrl + Shift + ~	Apply General format
Ctrl + Shift + $	Apply Currency format
Ctrl + Shift + %	Apply Percentage format
Ctrl + Shift + ^	Apply Exponential (Scientific) format
Ctrl + Shift + #	Apply Date format
Ctrl + Shift + @	Apply Time format
Ctrl + Shift + !	Apply Number format with commas and 2 decimal places
Ctrl + Shift + &	Apply border to selected cells
Ctrl + Shift + _	Remove border from selected cells
Alt + E, S, V	Open Paste Special dialog (legacy Excel menu access)
Ctrl + Alt + V	Open Paste Special dialog
Ctrl + Alt + F9	Force full calculation of all formulas

Shortcut	Action
F4 (after editing formula)	Cycle through absolute/relative references (A1, A$1, etc.)
Ctrl + Shift + U	Expand or collapse the formula bar

Copy, Cut, Paste, and Paste Special

These shortcuts help you **move** and **duplicate data** more efficiently, using both standard and special paste options. Mastering these is crucial for speeding up your workflow.

Shortcut	Action
Ctrl + C	Copy selected cells
Ctrl + X	Cut selected cells
Ctrl + V	Paste contents
Ctrl + Alt + V	Open Paste Special dialog
Alt + E, S, V	Legacy shortcut to open Paste Special (Excel 2003-style menu)
Ctrl + D	Fill down (copy from cell above)

Shortcut	Action
Ctrl + R	Fill right (copy from cell to the left)
Ctrl + ' (apostrophe)	Copy formula from cell above
Ctrl + Shift + "	Copy value from cell above
Ctrl + Shift + V (custom)*	Paste Values only (*Works in Excel 365 with customized shortcuts)
Alt + E, S, V	Paste Values (from Paste Special menu)
Alt + E, S, F	Paste Formulas only
Alt + E, S, T	Paste Formats only
Alt + E, S, C	Paste Comments only
Alt + E, S, N	Paste Validation only
Alt + E, S, W	Paste Column Widths only
Alt + E, S, L	Paste Links
Alt + E, S, M	Paste with Multiply
Alt + E, S, D	Paste with Divide
Alt + E, S, R	Paste with Transpose option

Shortcut	Action
Ctrl + Alt + F	Open Clipboard Task Pane (shows multiple copied items)
F4 (after a paste)	Repeat the last action (helpful with repeated pasting)

Note: The Alt + E, S, ... shortcuts are from the old Excel menu system, but they still work in modern Excel versions and are incredibly handy once memorized.

Undo, Redo, and Repeats

These shortcuts help you **quickly reverse or repeat your recent actions** — essential for efficient trial and error, editing, and data manipulation.

Shortcut	Action
Ctrl + Z	Undo the last action
Ctrl + Y	Redo the previously undone action
F4	Repeat the last command or action*
Ctrl + Shift + Z	Redo (in some Excel versions/macOS)

Shortcut	Action
Ctrl + Y	Redo typing, formatting, insert/delete
F4 (after action)	Repeats actions like insert row, format

Tip: The F4 key is one of the most powerful repeat tools in Excel. For example, if you bold a cell, then select another cell and press F4, it will also bold it.

Note for Mac Users: On macOS, **Cmd + Z** is Undo and **Cmd + Y** or **Cmd + Shift + Z** is Redo.

Formatting Cells and Ranges

These shortcuts help you quickly **apply number formats, align content, adjust font styles, add borders**, and access formatting menus — boosting your spreadsheet design game.

Shortcut	Action
Ctrl + 1	Open the Format Cells dialog
Ctrl + B	Apply or remove **bold** formatting
Ctrl + I	Apply or remove *italic* formatting
Ctrl + U	Apply or remove *underline*
Alt + H, F, F	Open font selector (Home > Font dropdown)

Shortcut	Action
Alt + H, F, S	Open font size selector
Ctrl + Shift + $	Apply Currency format
Ctrl + Shift + %	Apply Percentage format
Ctrl + Shift + #	Apply Date format
Ctrl + Shift + @	Apply Time format
Ctrl + Shift + ^	Apply Scientific format
Ctrl + Shift + !	Apply Number format with two decimals and commas
Ctrl + Shift + ~	Apply General number format
Ctrl + 5	Apply or remove strikethrough
Alt + H, A, C	Center align selected content
Alt + H, A, L	Align content left
Alt + H, A, R	Align content right
Alt + H, M, M	Merge & center selected cells
Alt + H, M, C	Merge cells only (without centering)
Alt + H, M, U	Unmerge cells
Alt + H, W	Wrap text within a cell
Alt + H, O, I	AutoFit column width
Alt + H, O, A	AutoFit row height
Alt + H, B, A	Add **all borders**
Alt + H, B, N	Remove all borders

Shortcut	Action
Ctrl + Shift + &	Add outline border to selected cells
Ctrl + Shift + _	Remove outline border from selected cells
Ctrl + 9	Hide selected rows
Ctrl + Shift + 9	Unhide hidden rows
Ctrl + 0	Hide selected columns
Ctrl + Shift + 0	Unhide hidden columns (*may need to be enabled in Windows settings*)
Alt + H, D, C	Delete selected column
Alt + H, D, R	Delete selected row
Alt + H, I, C	Insert column
Alt + H, I, R	Insert row

🔍 **Pro Tip**: Many of the Alt-based shortcuts follow the Ribbon path (Alt → H for Home, then next letters for features). Once you learn a few, they're super intuitive!

Row and Column Shortcuts

These shortcuts help you efficiently **insert, delete, select, hide, and unhide** rows and columns — super helpful for managing data layout.

Shortcut	Action
Ctrl + Space	Select entire column
Shift + Space	Select entire row
Ctrl + Shift + "+"	Insert new row or column (based on selection)
Ctrl + - (minus)	Delete selected row or column
Ctrl + 0	Hide selected column
Ctrl + Shift + 0	Unhide column (*may require enabling in Windows settings*)
Ctrl + 9	Hide selected row
Ctrl + Shift + 9	Unhide hidden row
Alt + H, I, R	Insert row
Alt + H, I, C	Insert column
Alt + H, D, R	Delete row
Alt + H, D, C	Delete column
Alt + O, C, A	AutoFit selected column(s)
Alt + O, R, A	AutoFit selected row(s)
Alt + H, O, I	AutoFit column width
Alt + H, O, A	AutoFit row height
Ctrl + Shift + Right Arrow	Extend selection to the last used column
Ctrl + Shift + Left Arrow	Extend selection to the first used column

Shortcut	Action
Ctrl + Shift + Down Arrow	Extend selection to the last used row
Ctrl + Shift + Up Arrow	Extend selection to the first used row
Ctrl + Arrow Keys	Jump to the edge of data region in a row/column

Pro Tip: Use Shift + Space to select a row before inserting or deleting — Excel knows what to do!

Worksheet & Workbook Management

These shortcuts help you **navigate, manage, insert, delete, rename, and switch between worksheets and workbooks** — crucial for power users working with multiple sheets or files.

Shortcut	Action
Ctrl + Page Down	Move to the next worksheet
Ctrl + Page Up	Move to the previous worksheet

Shortcut	Action
Shift + F11	Insert a new worksheet
Alt + Shift + F1	Insert new worksheet (alternate shortcut)
Ctrl + F4	Close the current workbook window
Ctrl + N	Create a new workbook
Ctrl + O	Open an existing workbook
Ctrl + S	Save the current workbook
F12	Open the "Save As" dialog
Ctrl + P	Open the Print dialog
Ctrl + Tab	Switch to the next open workbook
Ctrl + Shift + Tab	Switch to the previous open workbook
Alt + E, L	Delete the current worksheet
Alt + H, O, R	Rename the current worksheet

Shortcut	Action
Alt + H, O, H	Change tab color of the worksheet
Alt + H, O, M	Move or copy worksheet
Ctrl + F6	Cycle through open Excel windows (workbooks)
Ctrl + W	Close the active workbook
Ctrl + F9	Minimize workbook window
Ctrl + F10	Maximize or restore workbook window

💡 **Tip**: Combine Ctrl + Page Up/Down with Shift to select multiple sheets — great for making changes across several tabs at once!

Formulas and Functions

These shortcuts help you **insert, edit, and manage formulas quickly**, whether you're a beginner or an advanced user working with complex functions.

Shortcut	Action
= (equal sign)	Start a formula in a selected cell

Shortcut	Action
Tab (after typing function)	Auto-complete a formula or function name
Ctrl + A (in formula)	Open the Function Arguments dialog after typing a function name
Shift + F3	Open the Insert Function dialog
Alt + =	AutoSum (insert the SUM() function)
Ctrl + ` (grave accent)	Show or hide formulas in the worksheet
Ctrl + Shift + Enter	Enter an array formula (Excel 2019 and earlier)
Enter	Complete a formula and move down one cell
Shift + Enter	Complete a formula and move up
Tab	Complete a formula and move to the right
Ctrl + Enter	Complete a formula and stay in the same cell
F2	Edit the active cell with the cursor at the end of the content
Shift + F9	Calculate the active worksheet only

Shortcut	Action
F9	Calculate all worksheets in all open workbooks
Ctrl + Alt + F9	Force calculate all worksheets in all open workbooks
Ctrl + Shift + U	Expand or collapse the formula bar
Ctrl + [	Jump to the cell referenced in a formula
Ctrl +]	Return from the referenced cell
Ctrl + Shift + {	Select all cells directly or indirectly referenced by formulas
Ctrl + Shift + }	Select all cells with formulas that reference the active cell
Ctrl + ' (apostrophe)	Copy the formula from the cell above
Ctrl + K	Insert a hyperlink (useful in formulas with HYPERLINK())

Pro Tip: Use F9 inside a formula (while editing) to **evaluate a selected part** — very useful for debugging complex formulas.

Data Entry and Autofill

These shortcuts speed up your **data entry**, help with **autofilling patterns**, and reduce repetitive typing — perfect for working efficiently with large datasets.

Shortcut	Action
Ctrl + ;	Insert current date
Ctrl + Shift + :	Insert current time
Ctrl + Enter	Fill the selected range with the current entry
Ctrl + D	Fill down (copy contents of the top cell in a selection downward)
Ctrl + R	Fill right (copy contents of the leftmost cell in a selection rightward)
Alt + Down Arrow	Open the AutoComplete dropdown list (for cells with dropdowns or history)
Ctrl + Shift + "	Copy the value from the cell above
Ctrl + ' (apostrophe)	Copy the formula from the cell above
Ctrl + E	Flash Fill (automatically fills values based on pattern recognition)
Alt + E, S, V	Paste special values

Shortcut	Action
Alt + E, S, F	Paste special formulas
Alt + E, S, T	Paste special formats
Alt + E, S, W	Paste column widths
Alt + E, S, C	Paste comments
Alt + E, S, N	Paste validation rules
Alt + H, F, I	Autofill series (from Fill drop-down in Home tab)
Alt + H, F, D	Fill down from the Home tab
Alt + H, F, R	Fill right from the Home tab

💡 **Pro Tip**: Use **Flash Fill (Ctrl + E)** to instantly clean or split data (like extracting first names from full names).

Find, Replace, and Go To

These shortcuts help you **search, replace, and jump to specific cells or data** with precision — especially handy in large worksheets.

Shortcut	Action
Ctrl + F	Open the **Find** dialog box
Ctrl + H	Open the **Replace** dialog box
Ctrl + G	Open the **Go To** dialog box
F5	Also opens the **Go To** dialog box
Ctrl + Shift + F4	Find previous match (when using Find/Replace)
Shift + F4	Find next match (when using Find/Replace)
Ctrl + \	Select cells in a column that don't match the active cell
Ctrl + Shift + \	Select cells in a row that don't match the active cell
Ctrl +]	Go to direct dependents of the active cell
Ctrl + [	Go to direct precedents of the active cell
F5 → Special	(Then choose options like blanks, constants, formulas, etc.)

Pro Tip: In the **Go To Special** dialog (F5 → Special), you can jump to cells with formulas, blanks, conditional formatting, and more—great for cleaning or auditing a sheet.

AutoFill, Flash Fill, and Series

These shortcuts help you **automate repetitive data entry**, generate sequences, and use intelligent pattern recognition with AutoFill and Flash Fill tools.

Shortcut	Action
Ctrl + E	Flash Fill – Automatically fill values based on recognized patterns
Ctrl + D	Fill Down – Copy the contents of the cell above
Ctrl + R	Fill Right – Copy the contents of the cell to the left
Alt + H, F, I	Open the Fill Series dialog box
Alt + H, F, D	Fill Down from Home tab ribbon
Alt + H, F, R	Fill Right from Home tab ribbon
Alt + H, F, S	Open the Fill Series (same as Alt + H, F, I)
Ctrl + Shift + "	Copy value from the cell above
Ctrl + ' (apostrophe)	Copy formula from the cell above

Shortcut	Action
Drag Fill Handle (Mouse)	AutoFill data, patterns, or formulas manually by dragging the corner of a cell
Double-click Fill Handle	AutoFill down based on adjacent data column

Pro Tip: Combine Flash Fill (Ctrl + E) with smart examples — like separating names or formatting phone numbers — to instantly clean up messy data.

Filtering and Sorting Data

These shortcuts help you **quickly filter, sort, and analyze data** — essential for working with large spreadsheets.

Shortcut	Action
Ctrl + Shift + L	Toggle AutoFilter on/off
Alt + Down Arrow	Open the AutoFilter dropdown menu for the selected column
Alt + A, T	Turn on AutoFilter (if not active)
Alt + A, C	Clear filters from selected column
Alt + D, F, F	Apply/remove AutoFilter (Excel legacy shortcut)
Alt + A, S, S	Sort A to Z

Shortcut	Action
Alt + A, S, D	Sort Z to A
Alt + A, S, F	Sort by cell color
Alt + A, S, O	Sort by font color
Alt + A, S, I	Sort by icon
Alt + A, R	Refresh (for PivotTables or external data sources)
Alt + A, Q	Clear all sorts
Alt + A, E	Open the Sort dialog box
Alt + A, M	Advanced Filter dialog (manual custom filtering)
Alt + A, G	Group data (outline view)
Alt + Shift + Left Arrow	Ungroup data
Alt + Shift + Right Arrow	Group data
Alt + Shift + → / ←	Group/Ungroup rows or columns
Ctrl + Shift + L	(Toggle filters)
Alt + A, S, S	(Sort A to Z)
Alt + Down Arrow	(Open filter dropdown)

💡 **Pro Tip**: After activating filters, use **Alt + Down Arrow** to access quick filter/sort actions for the column your cursor is in.

Tables (Excel Structured Tables)

These shortcuts help you **create, navigate, and manage Excel Tables (also known as Structured Tables)** efficiently — perfect for organizing dynamic data ranges.

Shortcut	Action
Ctrl + T	Create a table from the selected data range
Ctrl + L	Also creates a table (legacy version of Ctrl + T)
Tab	Move to the next cell within the table row
Shift + Tab	Move to the previous cell within the table row
Ctrl + Space	Select the entire column within a table
Shift + Space	Select the entire row within a table
Ctrl + A	Select the entire table (when active cell is inside a table)

Shortcut	Action
Ctrl + Shift + Right Arrow	Select all columns of the table (when inside table)
Ctrl + Shift + Down Arrow	Select all rows of the table (when inside table)
Alt + J, T	Activate the **Table Design** tab
Alt + J, T, R	Rename the table (from the Table Design tab)
Alt + J, T, M	Add a total row to the bottom of the table
Alt + J, T, S	Toggle table style options (like banded rows, filter buttons)
Alt + H, O, I	AutoFit column width to content (applies to table columns too)
Ctrl + Shift + L	Toggle Filter buttons (on table headers)
Ctrl + Shift + 7	Apply outline border to selected table cells

 Pro Tip: Once your data is in a table, use structured references like =SUM(Table1[Sales]) for clearer and dynamic formulas.

31

PivotTables

These shortcuts help you **create, navigate, and manipulate PivotTables,** enabling you to analyze large data sets quickly and efficiently.

Shortcut	Action
Alt + N, V	Open the PivotTable creation wizard
Alt + D, P	Open the Legacy PivotTable and PivotChart Wizard
Ctrl + Shift + * (asterisk)	Select the entire PivotTable (when active cell is inside it)
Alt + J, T	Activate the PivotTable Analyze tab (Excel 365/2019+)
Alt + J, Y	Activate the PivotTable Tools > Analyze tab (older versions)
Alt + J, T, F	Refresh the PivotTable
Alt + F5	Refresh only the selected PivotTable
Ctrl + Alt + F5	Refresh all PivotTables and data connections
Alt + Shift + Right Arrow	Expand a collapsed PivotTable item
Alt + Shift + Left Arrow	Collapse an expanded PivotTable item

Shortcut	Action
Alt + Down Arrow	Open the filter dropdown in a PivotTable field
Alt + J, T, C	Clear the PivotTable
Alt + J, T, W	Move PivotTable to a new worksheet
Alt + J, T, L	Show or hide the field list
Tab	Move forward through fields in PivotTable
Shift + Tab	Move backward through fields in PivotTable
Ctrl + - (minus)	Remove selected field/item from PivotTable
Ctrl + Z	Undo the last PivotTable action

Pro Tip: Use Alt + D, P to access the classic PivotTable Wizard if you're combining multiple ranges or need advanced control.

Charts and Graphs

These shortcuts make it easy to **insert, format, and manage charts and graphs** to visually represent your data.

Shortcut	Action
Alt + F1	Create an **embedded chart** of the selected data in the current worksheet
F11	Create a **chart sheet** with the selected data
Ctrl + 1	Open the **Format Chart** (or Format Object) dialog box
Delete	Delete selected chart element or entire chart
Arrow Keys	Move selected chart element (e.g., legend, axis)
Ctrl + Arrow Keys	Resize chart elements (when selected)
Tab	Cycle through chart elements
Shift + Tab	Cycle through chart elements in reverse order
Enter	Select current chart element (after using Tab)
Ctrl + C	Copy chart or chart element
Ctrl + V	Paste chart or chart element

Shortcut	Action
Ctrl + X	Cut chart or chart element
Alt + J, C	Activate the **Chart Design** tab
Alt + J, F	Activate the **Format** tab for charts
Alt + J, C, T	Change chart type
Alt + J, C, A	Add chart element (titles, labels, gridlines, etc.)
Alt + J, C, L	Move chart to a different location or sheet
Alt + J, C, R	Switch row/column data in chart
Alt + J, C, D	Select different chart data
Alt + J, C, H	Change chart layout
Alt + J, C, S	Save as template

💡 **Pro Tip**: You can also right-click chart elements and use context menus — but these keyboard shortcuts are faster once you get the hang of them!

Named Ranges

Named ranges allow you to refer to specific cells or cell ranges with easy-to-remember names, making formulas clearer and spreadsheets more organized. Here's how to manage them efficiently with keyboard shortcuts:

Shortcut	Action
Ctrl + F3	Open the **Name Manager** to create, edit, or delete named ranges
Ctrl + Shift + F3	Create names from **selected row and/or column labels**
F3	Open the **Paste Name** dialog box to insert an existing named range
Alt + M, N	Create a new name using the **Name box** (via the Ribbon)
Alt + M, D	Define a name for a selected range (brings up the New Name dialog)
Alt + M, M	Open the **Name Manager** (same as Ctrl + F3, via Ribbon)
=Name	Type a formula directly using a named range (just start typing the name)

💡 **Note**: Named ranges can be used across worksheets and make complex formulas easier to read and audit.

Power Query and Data Tools

Power Query and data tools help automate, clean, transform, and connect to various data sources. These shortcuts streamline that process.

⬅ **Power Query Editor Shortcuts (Inside Power Query Window)**

Shortcut	Action
Ctrl + T	Convert selected data to a Table before loading to Power Query
Alt + A, P, T	Launch **Power Query Editor** (via Get & Transform → Launch Editor)
Ctrl + Space	Select the current column
Shift + Space	Select the current row
Ctrl + Click	Select multiple non-adjacent rows/columns
Ctrl + Shift + +	Insert a new step in the query
Ctrl + Z	Undo last action
Ctrl + Y	Redo an undone action
Delete	Delete selected step, row, or column
F2	Rename selected column or query
Home → Close & Load	(Alt + H, L) – Load data back to Excel worksheet

Shortcut	Action
Alt + Enter	Open **Advanced Editor** (to view/edit M code)
Alt + Down Arrow	Open filter menu in Power Query
Ctrl + A	Select all in a column or area

✎ General Data Tools (Outside Power Query)

Shortcut	Action
Alt + A, E	Open **Text to Columns** wizard
Alt + A, F, F	Apply or remove a **Filter**
Alt + A, S, S	Open **Sort** dialog box
Alt + A, M	**Remove Duplicates** from selected data
Alt + A, T	Open **Data Validation** dialog box
Alt + A, R	Refresh all data connections
Ctrl + Alt + F5	Refresh all connections and PivotTables
Alt + A, C	Consolidate data

Shortcut	Action
Alt + A, G	Group data
Alt + A, U	Ungroup data
Alt + D, F, F	Enable auto-filter (legacy shortcut)

💡 **Note**: Power Query Editor has limited shortcut coverage, but many actions still follow Windows UI logic (like Tab/Shift + Tab for navigation).

Data Validation and Protection

These shortcuts help you set rules for data entry, lock cells, and secure your worksheet or workbook.

Shortcut	Action
Alt + A, V, V	Open the **Data Validation** dialog box
Alt + D, L	Legacy shortcut to open **Data Validation**
Alt + Down Arrow	Open a drop-down list in a validated cell
Ctrl + 1	Open **Format Cells** dialog (for checking cell lock status)

You can use the **Data Validation dialog** to set rules (whole number, list, date, etc.), input messages, and error alerts.

Protection Shortcuts

Shortcut	Action
Alt + R, P, S	**Protect Sheet** – restrict edits with a password
Alt + R, P, W	**Protect Workbook** – prevent structure changes like renaming sheets
Alt + R, U, S	**Unprotect Sheet** (if protection is applied)
Alt + R, U, W	**Unprotect Workbook**
Ctrl + 1	Open **Format Cells** – go to **Protection tab** to lock/unlock cells
Ctrl + Shift + F or Ctrl + 1	Access **Format Cells** → **Protection** quickly

Note: Locking a cell does nothing unless the worksheet is also protected.

Macros and VBA Developer Tools

Macros help automate repetitive tasks, and the Developer tools let you write or edit VBA (Visual Basic for Applications) code. Here are the essential shortcuts to manage them efficiently:

🤖 Macro Shortcuts

Shortcut	Action
Alt + F8	Open the **Macro dialog box** (Run, Edit, or Delete Macros)
Alt + F11	Open the **VBA Editor (Visual Basic for Applications)**
Alt + F11 (again)	Toggle between VBA Editor and Excel
Alt + F4	Close the **VBA Editor**
Ctrl + Shift + R	Run the last executed macro (custom keyboard shortcut setup required)
Alt + T, M, R	Record a **new Macro**
Alt + T, M, M	Open **Macro dialog box** (same as Alt + F8)
Alt + T, M, E	Open **Macro Editor** (same as Alt + F11)

💡 **Tip**: When recording a macro, Excel lets you assign your own keyboard shortcut (e.g., Ctrl + Shift + a letter).

41

VBA Development Shortcuts (Inside the VBA Editor)

Shortcut	Action
F5	Run selected macro or code
F8	Step through code line-by-line
Shift + F2	Go to the definition of a variable or function
Ctrl + R	View the **Project Explorer**
Ctrl + G	Open the **Immediate Window**
Ctrl + F	Open **Find dialog** in the VBA editor
Ctrl + H	Open **Replace dialog** in VBA editor
Ctrl + Space	Trigger **IntelliSense** (auto-complete suggestions)
Ctrl + J	List all properties and methods

Shortcut	Action
Ctrl + Shift + F2	Jump back to the last edited location
Alt + Q	Close the **VBA Editor** and return to Excel

⚙ These are essential for anyone customizing Excel through VBA scripting and automation.

Review (Spellcheck, Comments, etc.)

These shortcuts help you **proofread, add notes**, and **collaborate effectively** in Excel.

📑 Spellcheck and Thesaurus

Shortcut	Action
F7	Run **Spellcheck**
Shift + F7	Open **Thesaurus**

💬 Tip: Spellcheck works one cell at a time; Excel checks the active cell or selected range.

💬 Comments (Modern Excel)

Shortcut	Action
Ctrl + Shift + F2	**Open the Comments pane** (Modern threaded comments)
Ctrl + Enter (in comment)	**Post a threaded comment** (Modern Excel versions)
Ctrl + Alt + M	**Insert a new comment** (Modern Excel)

Shortcut	Action
Alt + R, C	Another shortcut to **Insert a comment**
Alt + R, A, C	**Edit comment**
Alt + R, D	**Delete comment**
Alt + R, N	**Next comment**
Alt + R, P	**Previous comment**
Esc	Exit comment mode

Excel distinguishes between **threaded comments** (used for discussions) and **notes** (used for annotations).

Notes (Legacy Comments)

Shortcut	Action
Shift + F2	**Insert or edit a note** (legacy comment)
Ctrl + Shift + O	Select cells with **notes**
Ctrl + Alt + P	**Show/hide** all notes

Notes are the old-style yellow pop-up boxes. Still useful for quick reminders!

Printing and Page Layout

Whether you're preparing a report or printing your spreadsheet, these shortcuts make the job faster and easier.

Printing Shortcuts

Shortcut	Action
Ctrl + P	**Open the Print Preview & Print**
Ctrl + Shift + F12	**Open the Print dialog box**
Alt + F, P	Go to **Print menu** from the File tab
Esc (from Print)	**Exit Print Preview**

Page Layout & Setup Shortcuts

Shortcut	Action
Alt + P, S, P	Set **Print Area**

Shortcut	Action
Alt + P, S, C	**Clear Print Area**
Alt + P, O	Open **Page Setup** dialog box
Alt + P, M	**Margins** menu
Alt + P, M, A	**Custom Margins**
Alt + P, O, I	**Orientation** (Portrait or Landscape)
Alt + P, O, S	Set **Paper Size**
Alt + P, I	**Insert Page Break**
Ctrl + Shift + Enter	**Force Print Preview refresh**

🔍 Page Break View / Print View

Shortcut	Action
Alt + W, I	Switch to **Page Break Preview**
Alt + W, P	Switch to **Page Layout View**
Alt + W, L	Switch to **Normal View**

Headers, Footers, and Gridlines

Shortcut	Action
Alt + N, H	**Insert Header & Footer**
Alt + P, H, G	Show/Hide **Gridlines** (for printing)
Alt + P, H, H	Show/Hide **Headings** (row/column labels)

For finer control, use the **Page Setup dialog box** (Alt + P, S, P) to adjust scaling, alignment, and more.

Hyperlinks and External Links

These shortcuts help you quickly **insert, open, edit, and remove** hyperlinks in your Excel worksheet.

Hyperlink Shortcuts

Shortcut	Action
Ctrl + K	**Insert or edit a hyperlink**
Enter (on link)	**Follow hyperlink**

Shortcut	Action
Ctrl + Click	**Open hyperlink** in browser
Alt + N, I	**Insert hyperlink** from Ribbon
Ctrl + Z	**Undo hyperlink** insertion

When inserting a hyperlink (Ctrl + K), you can link to:

- A webpage
- An email address
- A file or folder
- Another place in the document

✖ Removing Hyperlinks

Shortcut	Action
Ctrl + Shift + F9	**Remove all hyperlinks** from selection
Right-click > Remove Hyperlink	**Remove selected hyperlink** (mouse action)

Note: Removing a hyperlink doesn't remove the text—just the link formatting and functionality.

Managing External Links

There's no direct shortcut key for managing external links, but you can access the relevant dialog quickly:

Shortcut	Action
Alt + A, K	**Edit Links** dialog (to manage external workbook links)
Alt + E, K	(Older Excel versions – same **Edit Links** dialog)

In the Edit Links dialog, you can update, change source, or break links to external workbooks.

Date & Time Entry

These shortcuts help you quickly enter the current **date** or **time** and manage datetime data with ease.

Entering Date and Time

Shortcut	Action
Ctrl + ;	**Insert current date**
Ctrl + Shift + ;	**Insert current time**
Ctrl + ; then Space then Ctrl + Shift + ;	**Insert current date and time**

These entries are **static** — they won't update like a formula.

⏱ Date & Time Functions (Using Formulas)

Shortcut	Function/Action
=TODAY()	Insert **today's date** (updates daily)
=NOW()	Insert **current date and time**

⏳ =TODAY() and =NOW() are **dynamic** — they recalculate whenever the sheet updates.

⬅ Quick Navigation with Date Entries

While not shortcuts in the typical sense, here are a couple of quick tips using the keyboard:

Action	Key/Tip
Auto-complete dates	Type part of a date, then press Enter
Fill series (dates)	Type a date, then drag fill handle
Ctrl + D / Ctrl + R	Copy dates down/right from above/left

Keyboard Tricks for Ribbon Navigation

These shortcuts help you **navigate, activate, and use** the Excel Ribbon efficiently with just your keyboard.

⚙ Activating and Navigating the Ribbon

Shortcut	Action
Alt	**Show Key Tips** (activates the Ribbon hotkeys)
Arrow Keys	Navigate between tabs or groups
Enter	Select the highlighted command

Shortcut	Action
Esc	Exit the Ribbon or cancel the command
F10	Also activates Key Tips (same as Alt)

Pressing Alt or F10 reveals letters on Ribbon tabs and commands. Press the corresponding letters to activate features.

● Ribbon Tab Access (After Pressing Alt)

Keys	Tab Accessed
Alt + H	Home tab
Alt + N	Insert tab
Alt + P	Page Layout tab
Alt + M	Formulas tab
Alt + A	Data tab
Alt + R	Review tab
Alt + W	View tab
Alt + F	File menu (Backstage view)
Alt + Q	Tell Me/Search

Keys	Tab Accessed
Alt + X	Add-ins tab (if enabled)
Alt + Y	Help tab (in newer Excel versions)

✗ Common Ribbon Commands (After Alt + Tab Key)

Once you activate a tab, you can continue typing letters to access specific commands. Here are some commonly used sequences:

Keys	Action
Alt + H, F, S	Font size drop-down
Alt + H, B	Borders menu
Alt + H, A, C	Center alignment
Alt + H, O, I	AutoFit column width
Alt + H, D, R	Delete row
Alt + A, T	Filter toggle
Alt + M, R	Insert function (fx)
Alt + P, S, P	Print preview

🔍 Tip: Use these in sequence — don't hold them down. Just press Alt, then H, then F, then S, for example.

🎖 Navigating the Ribbon with Add-ins or Custom Tabs

If you've installed add-ins or created custom tabs, they'll also get their own hotkeys (like Alt + X, Alt + Y, etc.). These will appear automatically when you press Alt.

Zooming, Views, and Window Management

These shortcuts help you quickly adjust **zoom levels**, switch **views**, and manage multiple **workbook windows**.

🔍 Zoom In and Out

Shortcut	Action
Ctrl + Mouse Scroll	Zoom in/out
Alt + W, Q	Open Zoom dialog box
Alt + V, Z	Open Zoom dialog (older Excel)

💡 Use the Zoom dialog to select a specific zoom percentage or fit selection.

🔳 Change Workbook Views

Shortcut	Action
Alt + W, L	Normal view
Alt + W, P	Page Layout view
Alt + W, I	Page Break Preview
Alt + W, F	Freeze Panes menu
Alt + W, S	Split window
Alt + W, G	Gridlines toggle
Alt + W, H	Headings toggle

🔳 Window Management Shortcuts

Shortcut	Action
Ctrl + F6	Switch to next open workbook window
Ctrl + Shift + F6	Switch to previous workbook window
Ctrl + Tab	Move to next open Excel window (Windows)

Shortcut	Action
Alt + W, N	New window of current workbook
Alt + W, A	Arrange all open windows
Alt + W, R	View side-by-side
Alt + W, T	Synchronous scrolling toggle
Ctrl + W	Close current window
Ctrl + O	Open a workbook

Excel for Mac (Shortcuts Variations)

💡 Excel Online (part of Microsoft 365) includes many of the same keyboard shortcuts as the desktop version, but there are **some differences** due to browser limitations.

📄 **Basic Navigation (Excel Online)**

Action	Shortcut
Move to next cell	Tab
Move to previous cell	Shift + Tab
Move to next row	Enter
Move to previous row	Shift + Enter

Action	Shortcut
Move one cell up/down/left/right	Arrow keys
Scroll down one screen	Page Down
Scroll up one screen	Page Up
Move to beginning of row	Home
Move to beginning of sheet	Ctrl + Home
Move to last cell with data	Ctrl + End

Cell Editing (Excel Online)

Action	Shortcut
Edit active cell	F2
Cancel cell entry	Esc
Enter and stay in same cell	Ctrl + Enter
Insert line break in cell	Alt + Enter

Action	Shortcut
Delete cell contents	Delete or Backspace

Copy, Paste, Cut

Action	Shortcut
Copy	Ctrl + C
Cut	Ctrl + X
Paste	Ctrl + V
Paste special (opens menu)	Ctrl + Alt + V
Fill down	Ctrl + D
Fill right	Ctrl + R

⬅ Undo / Redo

Action	Shortcut
Undo	Ctrl + Z
Redo	Ctrl + Y

🔍 Find and Replace

Action	Shortcut
Find	Ctrl + F
Replace	Ctrl + H

Formatting (Excel Online)

Action	Shortcut
Bold	Ctrl + B
Italic	Ctrl + I
Underline	Ctrl + U
Center align	Alt + H + A + C
Left align	Alt + H + A + L

Action	Shortcut
Right align	Alt + H + A + R
Format as number	Ctrl + Shift + 1
Format as currency	Ctrl + Shift + 4
Format as percent	Ctrl + Shift + 5
Format as scientific	Ctrl + Shift + 6

Worksheet / File Management (Web)

Action	Shortcut
Save workbook	Ctrl + S
Open workbook	Ctrl + O
Print workbook	Ctrl + P
Open context menu	Shift + F10
Rename worksheet (context menu)	Alt + H + O + R

Action	Shortcut
Insert worksheet	Shift + F11

Insert Elements

Action	Shortcut
Insert chart	Alt + F1
Insert hyperlink	Ctrl + K
Insert function	Shift + F3

Excel Online / Web Shortcuts

Here's a complete list of **Excel for Mac shortcut variations**, which are essential for Mac users who want to work efficiently in Excel. While many shortcuts are similar to Windows, Mac uses the **Command (⌘), Control (^), Option (⌥), and Shift** keys in place of Ctrl and Alt.

These are the **most important and correct Mac equivalents** of commonly used Excel shortcuts.

✳ Basic Navigation (Mac)

Shortcut	Action
⌘ + Arrow Keys	Move to edge of data region
Fn + Left Arrow	Home
Fn + Right Arrow	End
Fn + Up Arrow	Page Up
Fn + Down Arrow	Page Down
⌘ + ↑ or ↓	Go to top or bottom of column

Cell Editing (Mac)

Shortcut	Action
Control + U	Edit active cell
⌘ + Return	Enter and stay in same cell
⌘ + Tab	Move to next open application window

Copy, Cut, Paste (Mac)

Shortcut	Action
⌘ + C	Copy
⌘ + X	Cut
⌘ + V	Paste
⌘ + Option + V	Paste Special
⌘ + Z	Undo
⌘ + Y	Redo

✏ Formatting and Alignment (Mac)

Shortcut	Action
⌘ + B	Bold
⌘ + I	Italic
⌘ + U	Underline
⌘ + 1	Format Cells dialog
Control + ⌘ + Arrow Keys	Align cell contents

Formulas and Functions (Mac)

Shortcut	Action
Shift + F3	Insert function
Shift + F9	Calculate active worksheet
Fn + F2	Edit cell (same as Control + U)

Shortcut	Action
⌘ + Shift + K	Insert a hyperlink

🔍 Find, Replace, and Navigation (Mac)

Shortcut	Action
⌘ + F	Find
⌘ + H	Replace
Control + G	Go To

📊 Charts and Tables (Mac)

Shortcut	Action
Fn + F11	Create chart
⌘ + T	Create Excel Table

Window and File Management (Mac)

Shortcut	Action
⌘ + N	New workbook
⌘ + O	Open workbook
⌘ + S	Save workbook
⌘ + P	Print
⌘ + W	Close window
⌘ + Q	Quit Excel

Miscellaneous (Mac)

Shortcut	Action
⌘ + K	Insert hyperlink
⌘ + , (comma)	Open Excel Preferences
Control + ⌘ + V	Paste Special
⌘ + Option + R	Refresh PivotTable

Note: Some function key shortcuts (F1–F12) may require you to use the **Fn key** on MacBooks depending on system settings.

Important Notes for Excel Online Users

- Some desktop shortcuts may be **partially supported** or behave differently.
- **Alt-based ribbon navigation (e.g., Alt + H + O + R)** works **after tapping Alt key** first.
- If you're using Excel in a browser on **Mac**, use **Command (⌘)** instead of Ctrl where applicable.

Accessibility Features

Here's a detailed list of **Accessibility Features** shortcuts in Excel (both Windows and Mac), designed to help you improved navigation, screen reading, and usability support. These shortcuts are particularly useful for users leveraging assistive technologies.

❋ **Windows Accessibility Shortcuts**

Shortcut	Action
Alt + Shift + A	Open Accessibility Checker
Alt + Q	Move focus to "Tell me what you want to do"
Ctrl + F6	Move between open workbooks or panes
F6	Cycle through screen elements in a worksheet or window
Shift + F6	Cycle backward through screen elements
Ctrl + Shift + F6	Cycle backward through open Excel windows
Ctrl + Tab	Move between worksheets when workbook is full screen
Alt + F10	Navigate to the Ribbon using the keyboard

Shortcut	Action
Tab	Move forward through options and commands
Shift + Tab	Move backward through options and commands
Enter	Activate selected command or option
Esc	Exit menus, dialog boxes, or cancel a command
Alt	Activate KeyTips (access Ribbon tabs with keyboard)
Alt + Down Arrow	Open a dropdown list
Ctrl + Alt + Spacebar	Activate a screen reader to read out selected cell
Windows + U	Open Windows Ease of Access settings

❄ Mac Accessibility Shortcuts

Shortcut	Action
Control + Option + Spacebar	Speak selected item (with VoiceOver enabled)
Control + Option + Right Arrow	Navigate to next UI element (VoiceOver)

Shortcut	Action
Control + Option + Left Arrow	Navigate to previous UI element
Control + Option + Command + H	Read entire worksheet
⌘ + Option + F5	Accessibility Options (macOS system-wide)
Fn + Control + F6	Cycle through panes in Excel
Control + F7	Move focus to menu bar (if full keyboard access enabled)
⌘ + ?	Open Excel Help

☑ **Tip:** Excel is compatible with **screen readers** like **Narrator (Windows)** or **VoiceOver (Mac)**. You can also use third-party tools like **JAWS** or **NVDA** with Excel.

⚙ **Enable Accessibility Checker in Excel**:
- **Windows**: File → Info → Check for Issues → Check Accessibility
- **Mac**: Tools → Check Accessibility

Custom Keyboard Shortcuts (for power users)

⚠ **Note**: Excel does not allow extensive *native* custom keyboard shortcut creation like some other apps (e.g., Photoshop or VS Code). However, **power users** can still assign or simulate custom shortcuts via:

- The **Quick Access Toolbar (QAT)**
- **Macros with assigned shortcut keys**
- Windows/Mac system tools
- Third-party apps like AutoHotKey (Windows) or Karabiner-Elements (Mac)

🛠 Customizing via Quick Access Toolbar (QAT) (Windows & Mac)

Steps	What It Does
Alt key (then 1–9, A–Z)	Activates commands added to the QAT in their order.
File → Options → QAT	Add frequently used commands to the QAT, then access them via Alt + QAT number.
Alt + Shift + [QAT number]	Customize the QAT command location quickly (Windows only).

Example: Add "Sort Ascending" to QAT and access it with Alt + 1.

⊞ Assigning Shortcuts to Macros

Action	Shortcut / How-to
Alt + F8	Open Macro dialog
Alt + F11	Open Visual Basic Editor
Ctrl + Shift + [Any Letter]	Assign this combo to a macro when saving it (in Macro Options dialog)
Tools → Macro → Macros (Mac)	Access macros and assign keys in Excel for Mac

Note: Use descriptive names and store macros in **Personal Macro Workbook** for global use across Excel files.

🖥 Using Windows Tools (Power Users)

Tool	What You Can Do
AutoHotKey	Remap any keyboard shortcut or create your own complex Excel workflow automations
PowerToys (Keyboard Manager)	Remap keys and shortcuts across the OS

Example AutoHotKey Script (Windows):

^!s::Send, ^+L ; Press Ctrl+Alt+S to apply currency format (Ctrl+Shift+L)

Mac Custom Shortcuts

Steps	Action
System Preferences → Keyboard → Shortcuts → App Shortcuts	Add custom keyboard shortcuts for Excel menu commands
⌘ + Option + [custom key] (example)	If assigned to a menu title (e.g., "Merge & Center")

⚠ For Mac: Custom shortcuts **must exactly match** the menu item's text in Excel (case sensitive).

Tips for Power Users
- Use the **Function Keys (F1–F12)** creatively: Assign macros or remap using OS tools.
- **Avoid overriding system-reserved keys** unless necessary.
- Keep a **cheat sheet** for your custom mappings.

www.ingramcontent.com/pod-product-compliance
Lightning Source LLC
LaVergne TN
LVHW051609050326
832903LV00033B/4413